```
J                    R564156
796.7                   11.90
Jef
Jefferis
The checkered flag
```

DATE DUE			

GREAT RIVER REGIONAL LIBRARY

St. Cloud, Minnesota 56301

THE CHECKERED FLAG

THE HISTORY OF RACING CARS

David Jefferis

Franklin Watts
New York London Toronto Sydney

Illustrated by
Peter Bull
Robert and Rhoda Burns
Chris Forsey
Ron Jobson
Michael Roffe

Photographs supplied by
Allsport
Mary Evans Picture Library
David Jefferis
National Motor Museum

Technical consultants
Robert Burns
Patrick Devereux

© 1991 Franklin Watts

Franklin Watts, Inc.
387 Park Avenue South
New York, NY 10016

Printed in Belgium

All rights reserved

Library of Congress Cataloging-in-Publication data

Jefferis, David
The checkered flag : the history of racing cars / David Jefferis.
p. cm – – (Wheels)
Summary: Surveys the world of automobile racing, discussing racing circuits, rallies, future racing cars, aerodynamics and technology, and Grand Prix winners.
ISBN 0–531–14122–5
1. Automobile racing – History – Juvenile literature.
2. Automobiles. Racing – History – Juvenile literature
[1. Automobile racing 2. Automobiles. Racing.] I. Jefferis. David. II. Title. III. Series: Wheels.
GV1029.15.L24 1991
796.7'2 – dc20

90-32128
CIP AC

THE CHECKERED FLAG

Contents

Introduction	4
The first races	6
Racing circuits	8
The "brickyard"	10
24 hours at Le Mans	12
The grand prix	14
Racing car design	16
At the wheel	18
Rally!	20
Racing to win	22
Future racers	24
Racing progress	26
Facts and records	28
Racing technology	30
Index	32

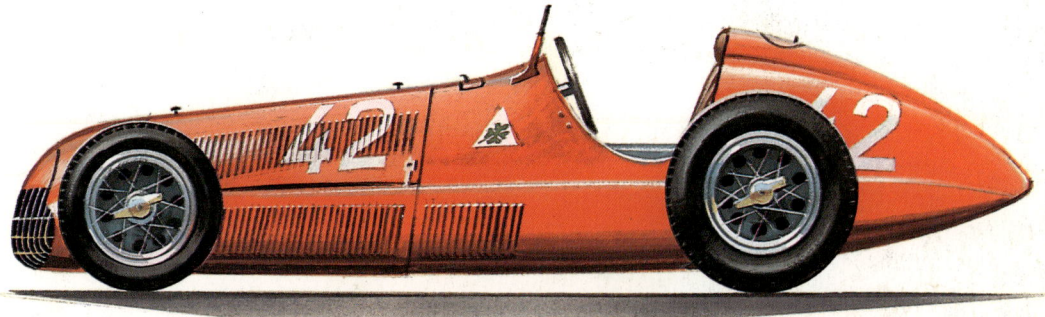

Introduction

People have been racing cars ever since the automobile was invented. The first car was built in 1885, and just ten years later the first official motor race took place on the open roads of France. Motor racing was established as an exciting sport, with international appeal.

The success of the early races soon encouraged the development of special racing cars, and different races, testing the drivers' skill and endurance. The first grand prix (literally "big prize") race was held in 1906. Different levels of racing car emerged, inspiring separate groups of races. These are known as formula races, after the formula – a set of special rules – that applies to the cars used in each type of race. The formula governs the dimensions and weight of the car, engine size and so on. Racing drivers usually graduate through the levels of formula racing. They start on the Formula Ford cars, using fairly cheap-to-race vehicles. If they prove successful, they move on to the more powerful Formula Three machines. The next step is to Formula 3000, and then, finally, to Formula One racing.

Graduating to Formula One, the arena of the world champions, is the great ambition. Some have reached the goal early. The youngest-ever world champion was Emerson Fittipaldi of Brazil who won in 1972 when he was just 25. On the other hand, Juan Fangio of Argentina took the checkered flag to win his last grand prix at the venerable age of 46, in 1957.

Drivers are often the heroes, but the great success of the sport depends on many others: the crowds of spectators; the car manufacturers; and the sponsors who fund the top racing teams to the tune of several million dollars a year.

◁ Safety is a top priority on today's race circuits. Behind this Benetton-Ford, driven by the Italian Alessandro Nannini, you can see a section of armco barrier, painted red and white. Armco is designed to absorb the impact of cars driven at high speed and to prevent them from crashing into spectators.

Motor racing century

These two racing cars cover a period of more than 80 years. During this time, car design, construction and performance have improved enormously. Early racers had open cockpits, there was little in the way of aerodynamic body shaping, and the large but inefficient engines gave them speeds that were quite low by today's standards.

1906 Renault

△ This Renault was driven to victory in the first grand prix race, held in 1906, at Le Mans in France. The car had a massive 12.9-liter engine and could reach over 100 km/h (62 mph). Its chassis (the frame to which engine, wheels and bodywork are attached) was made of steel. This was lighter and stronger than the wooden chassis, used on most other cars of the time.

▽ The 1990 McLaren-Honda MP4/5B is a typical modern Formula One design, with a one-piece chassis including a protective bath-tub-shaped section for the driver's seat.

1990 McLaren-Honda

The first races

The first motor race was held in France in 1895. The course was a round trip on the roads between the cities of Paris and Bordeaux. Emile Levassor won the race, driving a French-built Panhard. He roared across the Paris finish line, having completed the 1,178 km (730 mile) race at an average speed of 24 km/h (15 mph) – a good result, since early automobiles were slow and unreliable.

In the next few years, motor racing became very popular, and many events were held. The roads then were not like the smooth, paved highways of today, however. Outside cities, they were mostly unsurfaced, and were dusty in summer and muddy in winter. Racing drivers had to take care, not only because of the difficult road surfaces, but also because spectators were inclined to wander into the road, failing to appreciate the speed of the cars thundering past. Stray animals were a constant hazard too!

There were so many crashes in the Paris to Madrid race of 1903 that the race organizers stopped the event at the end of the first day's racing. Among the dead drivers was Marcel Renault, one of the early founders of the Renault car company. Marcel's brother, Louis, another driver, retired from motor racing as soon as he heard the news of his brother's death. Today, however, the Renault car company is a major force in motor sport.

The heroine of the Paris-Madrid race was Madame du Gast, the only woman to enter. She pulled off the road to give first aid treatment to other drivers who had been hurt in accidents during the race.

△ Emile Levassor and his mechanic, in the triumphant 1895 Panhard. Twenty-two vehicles started out in the Paris-Bordeaux-Paris race. Fifteen had gasoline engines, six were steam powered. One had an electric motor, but broke down soon after the start.

△ Louis Renault, driving the red car, passes a Dietrich in the 1903 Paris-Madrid race. On the one and only day of the race, the leaders averaged over 105 km/h (65 mph). But the organizers were so shocked by the number of accidents that they ordered all cars to be returned to Paris by train.

▽ Steam cars were quite common in the early days of racing, and many, such as this 1905 White steam car, were entered in motor races.

△ Refueling a Fiat in the French Grand Prix of 1912. The fuel tank was behind the driver's seat. In a crash, the tank could easily split and leak fuel. Today's cars have self-sealing tanks, to prevent fuel spills in all but the worst accidents.

Racing circuits

The disasters of the Paris-Madrid race finished open-road racing in Europe. Race organizers realized that to allow fast cars to race on roads that were in everyday use was asking for trouble. The answer to the problem was quite simple however; they decided that races should be held on circuits of quiet roads, which would be closed off to other traffic for as long as the race was in progress. This applied to both big and small races. Even the Gordon Bennett Cup, which was the most important event of its time, was held on closed-off roads after 1903. Outside Europe, open-road racing was phased out.

In 1904, the first Vanderbilt Cup races were held on Long Island, in New York. Here too, the cars raced on closed-road circuits. By 1906 however, conditions were again excessively dangerous. More than 250,000 people crowded onto the 48 km (30 mile) circuit to watch the race. As French driver Louis Wagner hurtled past the winning post in his Darracq, only superb driving skills enabled him to avoid mowing down many spectators who crowded onto the track.

Once closed-road racing was established, special racing tracks were designed. The first was built in Britain, not far from London. This 4.3 km (2.7 mile) circuit, Brooklands, featured spectacular banking on the bends. Roaring along the concrete surface, cars could reach speeds of nearly 200 km/h (125 mph) up on the banked curves, even more down the straights. Brooklands remained the centre of British motor racing until 1939. Today it is no longer used for racing, but parts of the track remain and visitors can still see the extraordinary banking from the woods surrounding much of the circuit.

◁ This early Mercedes-Benz had a huge engine and a top speed of more than 160 km/h (100 mph). In 1908, Christian Lautenschlager, the Mercedes-Benz chief test driver, won the Dieppe Grand Prix in the car. Four years later, in 1912, Italian-American driver Ralph De Palma won the Vanderbilt Cup in a similar car.

◁ Neck-and-neck at Brooklands in the 1920s. Built in 1906, the track was used for many important races. The first driver to complete a lap at 193 km/h (120 mph) was K. Lee Guiness, who was awarded a special badge after his effort during a race in 1924. The banking of the track helped early cars whose tires and suspension could not easily absorb the sideways force generated when cornering at speed. The tilted track allowed them to "lean over" on the bends, like bicycles or motorcycles.

Modern tracks

Grand prix racing takes place at circuits all over the world. The season lasts from March to November and takes in some 16 races. The driver who gains the most points becomes world champion for the year.

△ The American circuit in Phoenix, Arizona, follows a route of closed-off city streets.

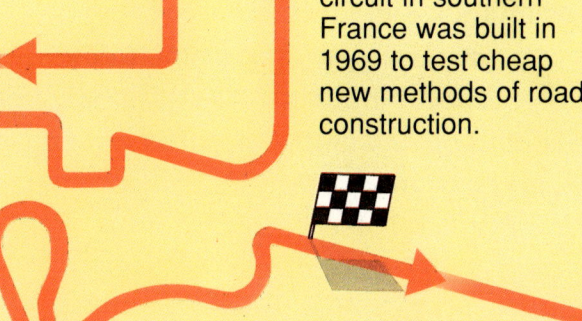

▽ The Paul Ricard circuit in southern France was built in 1969 to test cheap new methods of road construction.

Direction of race
Start/finish

△ Built on an old World War II bomber base, Britain's Silverstone offers high speed racing on its flat, 5.15-km (3.2 mile) course. A grand prix race here lasts for a total of 64 laps.

△ Another street circuit, this time in Adelaide, Australia. The roads are wide and the speeds high. 320 km/h (200 mph) is possible on the circuit's longest straight.

The "brickyard"

Before World War I, the city of Indianapolis, Indiana, was a major car-making center. Local businessman Carl Fisher decided that the bumpy streets of the city were not fit to display the high performance of vehicles turned out by the local car factories. His idea was to build a speedway on which cars could be demonstrated running smoothly, as fast as they could go. In the spring of 1909, his plan went into action. Workers laid out a 4 km (2.5 mile) circuit. It was simple enough as race tracks go, with two long and two short straights joined by four curved corners, but the first race program was a disaster. The tires of the cars and motorcycles were torn to shreds by the crushed rock and tar track surface, and several fatal accidents put a stop to the racing. Rebuilding work started in October 1909, and on December 10, after 63 days of hard labor, the new track was completed. It consisted of a bed of sand laid over the old track, topped by 3,200,000 bricks. Ever since, the Indianapolis Speedway has been known as the "brickyard."

The most famous race at the brickyard is the Indianapolis 500. Carl Fisher decided on a 800 km (500 mile) event, which he billed as "the most demanding speed contest yet devised." In the first race, 40 cars lined up on the starting line, among them a Marmon driven by Ray Harroun, who had designed the vehicle as a single-seater. Most racing cars of the time had two seats, one for the driver, the other for a mechanic, who also served as a look-out to warn the driver of anyone trying to overtake. Other competitors complained that Harroun might be a danger if he couldn't see behind him to check for cars overtaking. To avoid possible disqualification, Harroun added a small rear-view mirror over the cockpit, and thus became the first person to use one on an automobile. He went on to win the race.

◁ Ray Harroun, driving the Marmon in 1911. It was some years before his rear-view mirror idea came into widespread use. Grand prix cars had to have mirrors installed after 1923.

△ Cars like this Duesenberg were typical of the "Indy" (Indianapolis) racers of the 1920s. The engine cover was kept shut with thick leather straps. As well as using the Indy track for racing, Duesenberg used it for testing ordinary passenger cars.

▽ Mechanics hurriedly check and refuel Rick Mears' car in the 1988 Indy 500. Near the pits is the starting line, marked by a single row of bricks, all that remains of the original all-brick surface. Today the track is laid with smooth tarmac.

11

24 hours at Le Mans

△ The fly-splattered nose of the winning Mercedes-Benz in the 1989 Le Mans race.

The 24-hour race at Le Mans in France is the world's longest road race. It is also by far the toughest, testing drivers and machines at speeds which reach nearly 400 km/h (250 mph).

The first Le Mans race was held in 1923 and won at an average speed of 92 km/h (57 mph). Speeds continued to increase until the 1955 event, which was a race of tragedy and triumph. In the third hour of the race, a Mercedes-Benz driven by Pierre Levegh struck an Austin-Healey, which came off the track and hit a French policeman. The Mercedes was catapulted into the air and crashed down onto a trackside safety embankment. It bounced off the bank and smashed into the crowd, spraying people with burning fuel and white-hot pieces of metal. Levegh and 82 spectators were killed, and 150 others were injured. In fact, this was the worst motor racing accident on record. The Mercedes-Benz team withdrew, but the race itself continued and driver Mike Hawthorn eventually won in his Jaguar D-type. After the race, the safety barriers at Le Mans were improved, and the distance between the track and the crowd increased. Many other circuits were also improved. Motor racing will never be risk-free, but a tragedy on the scale of the 1955 race is unlikely to happen again.

60 years of Le Mans winners

These cars are among the most famous in the history of the Le Mans endurance race.

▷ Bentleys were winners in the 1920s and 1930s. This one was claimed to have a top speed of 217 km/h (135 mph).

▽ In 1966, Ford GT40s took the first three places. Fords won at Le Mans for the next three years.

△ The Jaguar C-type won Le Mans in 1951 and 1953. The improved D-type, shown here, went on to win the race in 1955, 1956 and 1957.

△ Porsche dominated sports car racing throughout the 1970s and 1980s. This 917 averaged 191 km/h (119 mph) to win the 1970 race.

▷ By the end of the 24-hour event, 1989's winning Mercedes had covered a total distance of 5,266 km (3,272 miles).

At various times in the history of the 24-hour race, different racing teams have dominated the track, often winning several years in a row. In the 1920s, British Bentleys took the checkered flag four times. Jaguars won races in the 1950s. In the 1960s it was Ford's turn. The company made a massive effort, spending millions of dollars to develop a race-winning vehicle.

The reward came in 1966, when Chris Amon and Bruce McLaren crossed the finish line in a Ford GT40. In 24 hours, they had covered 4,842 km (3,009 miles) at an average speed of 202 km/h (125 mph). Ford cars won again in the following three years.

The 1970s and early 1980s were great years for Porsche, but Jaguar has returned to win the 1988 and 1990 races.

13

The grand prix

The first grand prix was held on the weekend of June 26-27, 1906, on a circuit near Le Mans. Six laps of the 103 km (64 mile) course were run on the first day, with a further six laps the next day.

The drivers blasted along under a hot sun, reaching speeds of nearly 160 km/h (100 mph) on the straights. Hungarian driver Ferenc Szisz, driving a Renault (shown on page 5), battled for first place with the Italian Felice Nazzaro, driving a Fiat. Szisz managed to take first place, partly because of the time he saved using a new type of detachable wheel rim. These allowed tires to be changed as complete units, quickly and easily. Only Renault, Fiat and Itala cars had these wheels. The other teams cut off worn tires with knives, mounting new tires and inflating them once they were on the car.

Today's grand prix racing cars have quick-change wheels, and a team of skilled mechanics can refuel a car, change all the wheels and install new brake pads in little more than a minute.

Though grand prix cars became increasingly powerful, the basic layout of a front-mounted engine and rear-wheel drive remained popular until the 1960s. Then, in 1962, there was a major design change. The Lotus 25 had a mid-mounted engine, with the driver sitting in a reclining position, and it had a "monocoque" chassis. This combined body and chassis as a single, strong unit, a system which was stronger and lighter than the earlier method of bodywork plus a heavy chassis "backbone." The reclining position meant the car could be lower, reducing air drag at high speed, and the mid-mounted engine position improved cornering. In 1962, Scotsman Jim Clark drove the Lotus to three grand prix victories. The following year he became world champion and the Lotus took the season's prize for best car. Since then, all modern racing cars have followed similar design principles to those of the Lotus 25.

▷ With its smooth bodywork removed, a racing car reveals its monocoque chassis. The single-shell structure is designed as a protective "bathtub", in which the driver sits, and which gives good protection in a crash. In theory, a driver can remove the steering wheel (seen here in front of the cockpit), snap off the seat belt, and be out of the car within five seconds.

△ The pits are where mechanics service and refuel cars during a race. The name dates back to the 1908 French Grand Prix, when real pits were dug so that mechanics could service their cars from underneath.

▷ Winners from three ages of grand prix racing. The 1924 Alfa Romeo P2 was designed, built and raced in only nine months, and proved highly successful. The Mercedes-Benz W196 of the 1950s came in two body styles, one of them designed for use on tracks with tight bends. A streamlined version was used on longer courses. The Lotus 25 was the first "modern" racer, with a layout that continues to inspire designers today.

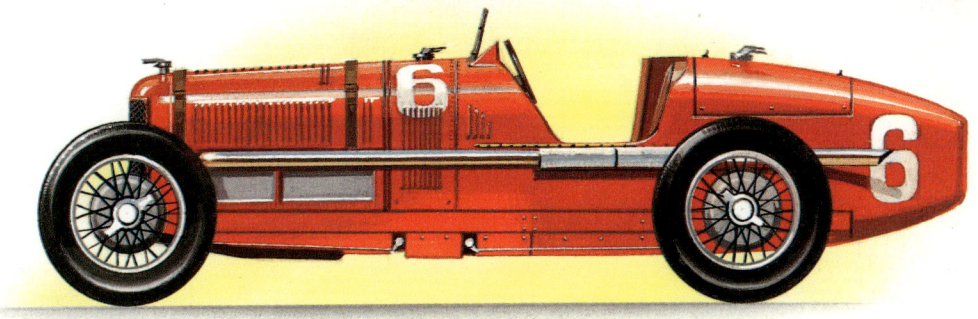

Alfa Romeo P2

Mercedes-Benz W196

Lotus 25

Racing car design

One of the major problems for designers is to create cars that stay firmly on the track at high speed, rather than becoming unstable and flipping into the air. Various solutions have been tried, but the most successful approach is the use of aerofoil wings and ground-effects body design. The wings act just like those of an aircraft, but in reverse – instead of lifting the car into the air, they push it downward, onto the track, a result known as downforce. Ground-effects design shapes the car body itself to produce downforce.

Meanwhile, turbo technology has increased the amount of power available from an engine. The turbo engine uses a small turbine wheel mounted in the exhaust system, which spins in the rush of exhaust gases, and pumps more air into the air intake. The result is a rush of extra power when the driver needs it. In fact, turbo engines produce so much extra power that only a few years after they were introduced, turbocharged cars won hands down against ordinary engines. At first, the rules were changed to give the turbos a handicap. But after the 1988 season, the rules were changed again, and turbos are no longer allowed in Formula One racing.

▽ The 1979 Renault RS 11 was the first turbocharged grand prix car to win a race.

▽ Some features of the Ferrari 640:
1 Front aerofoil wings.
2 Slim nose section of monocoque body.
3 Wide tires to give maximum grip.
4 Wheels that can be changed in seconds.
5 Wide side-sections housing air ducts for the engine. Fuel is stored behind the driver.
6 Ferrari V12 engine.
7 Rear tires, even larger than front ones.
8 Cockpit, tailor-made for each driver.
9 Rear aerofoil wing.
10 When empty, the car weighs 500 kg (1,100 lb).

◁ The Brabham-Alfa Romeo BT46B of 1978 used a large fan for engine cooling. The fan also took air from under the car and, like a giant vacuum cleaner, sucked the Brabham down onto the track. After Niki Lauda won the Swedish Grand Prix in the car, it was banned from racing, as the fan was considered something of a cheat.

This car was driven by British driver Nigel Mansell during the 1989 racing season.

△ A look inside the cockpit of a grand prix racing car, a tight fit for any driver.

At the wheel

Before climbing into the cockpit, a driver has to get dressed. Layers of undergarments are put on first, followed by fireproof overalls, gloves and boots. The outfit is completed by a balaclava, worn under a helmet which can be plugged into an emergency oxygen supply, and a two-way radio to talk to the pit crew.

All this has to be worn, no matter how hot the weather. Most of it gives protection in case of a crash. But clothing that is designed to ward off fire also keeps heat in the rest of the time. With an engine behind the seat, four sets of brakes that work at 750-930°F, and oil and water coolers running at 195-212°F, it's hot in the tight-fitting cockpit. So hot, in fact, that in warm weather a driver can easily sweat away 3 kg (7 lb) during the course of a single two-hour race.

A seat belt keeps the driver strapped firmly in the seat. A mechanic has to tighten it, as there is no room in the cockpit for the driver to secure it properly. Closed sports cars, such as those used at Le Mans, have cramped cockpits too. In 1967, the Ford GT40 driven by Dan Gurney had to have a bulge made in its roof to provide enough headroom for him.

In front of the driver is the small, removable steering wheel. It is heavy to turn at slow speeds, as the tires are big and there is no power assistance. The set of instruments includes temperature and oil pressure gauges and the tachometer, which indicates engine speed. The stubby gear lever is on the right, while accelerator, brake and clutch pedals are down at the driver's feet.

△ Though many safety precautions are taken, crashes still occur on the track. If a car lands upside down, its roll hoop is designed to save the driver's neck.

▷ This Jaguar is an unusual high-speed fire engine. Replacing its back seat is a pump and a large tank of fire-quenching foam.

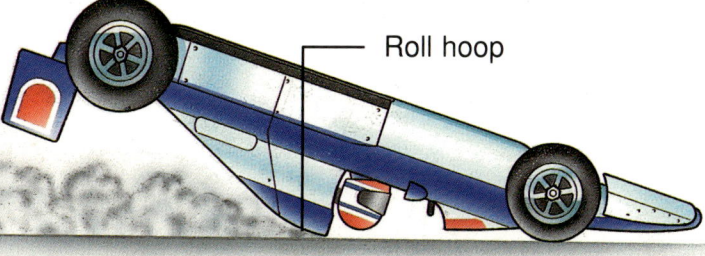

Roll hoop

▷ Track safety is the responsibility of the track marshal team, mostly volunteers who do the job because they love the world of motor racing. Marshals use various flags to signal drivers during the course of a race.
1 Warns of an overtaking car.
2 Warns of danger on the track ahead.
3 Warns of a slippery track, probably oil.
4 Warns of a service vehicle on the track.
5 Track is now all clear.
6 Orders all cars to stop at once.
7 Waved to the winner at the finish line.

19

Rally!

Rallies are feats of endurance, which test cars and crews over long distances and through different types of country, often over very difficult terrain.

Competitors start off at intervals of about a minute, aiming to travel on a given route to arrive at daily checkpoints at the precise times given by the organizers of the rally. Teams lose points if they are late, or if they are early too, though the bigger rallies have special off-road sections, where speed alone is what counts. On these sections, and wherever the going gets difficult, cars with four-wheel drive have an advantage. Power on all the wheels helps cornering and grip, especially on rough or muddy surfaces.

The 1990 Safari Rally, held on 4,200 km (2,600 miles) of Kenyan dirt tracks, was a battle for first place between the four-wheel drive cars of the Italian Lancia and Japanese Toyota teams. Conditions were the worst in many years, with heavy rain creating unusually slimy conditions. World rally champion Massimo Biasion ended his hope for victory in the race when he drove his Lancia Delta Integrale straight into a deep mud hole. Spanish driver Carlos Sainz crashed into a tree. Though the car took several hours to be repaired, Sainz was unhurt, and carried on to take fourth place after listening to the advice from local bystanders. "Pole-pole" they urged him, the Swahili word for "slow down!"

The winner of the six-day rally was Scandinavian driver Bjorn Waldegard, in a four-wheel drive Toyota GT-4. He was lucky as well as skillful – earlier in the rally, one unfortunate driver parked his car at the side of the muddy road, only to watch it slide straight into a ditch!

◁ The first long rally was held between China and France in 1907. The 12,000 km (7,500 mile) event was won by an Italian, Prince Scipione Borghese, who arrived in Paris on August 10, two months after leaving Peking. A similar event was held in 1990, but in the opposite direction, from London to Peking. Teams from many countries took part in the rally.

▽ The Ford Cosworth rally car has a range of specially fitted equipment. This includes lightweight seats, a built-in fire extinguisher, extra lights, navigation equipment and a very powerful engine, which can catapult the car from 0-100 km/h (60 mph) in five seconds.

△ Takeoff for a Lancia Delta, as it hurtles through the dust and dirt of the Safari Rally. Four-wheel drive machines are the only winners in these tough events. Vehicles with two-wheel drive are left far behind when the going gets difficult.

▽ Two of today's most successful rally cars.

Lancia Delta

Toyota GT-4

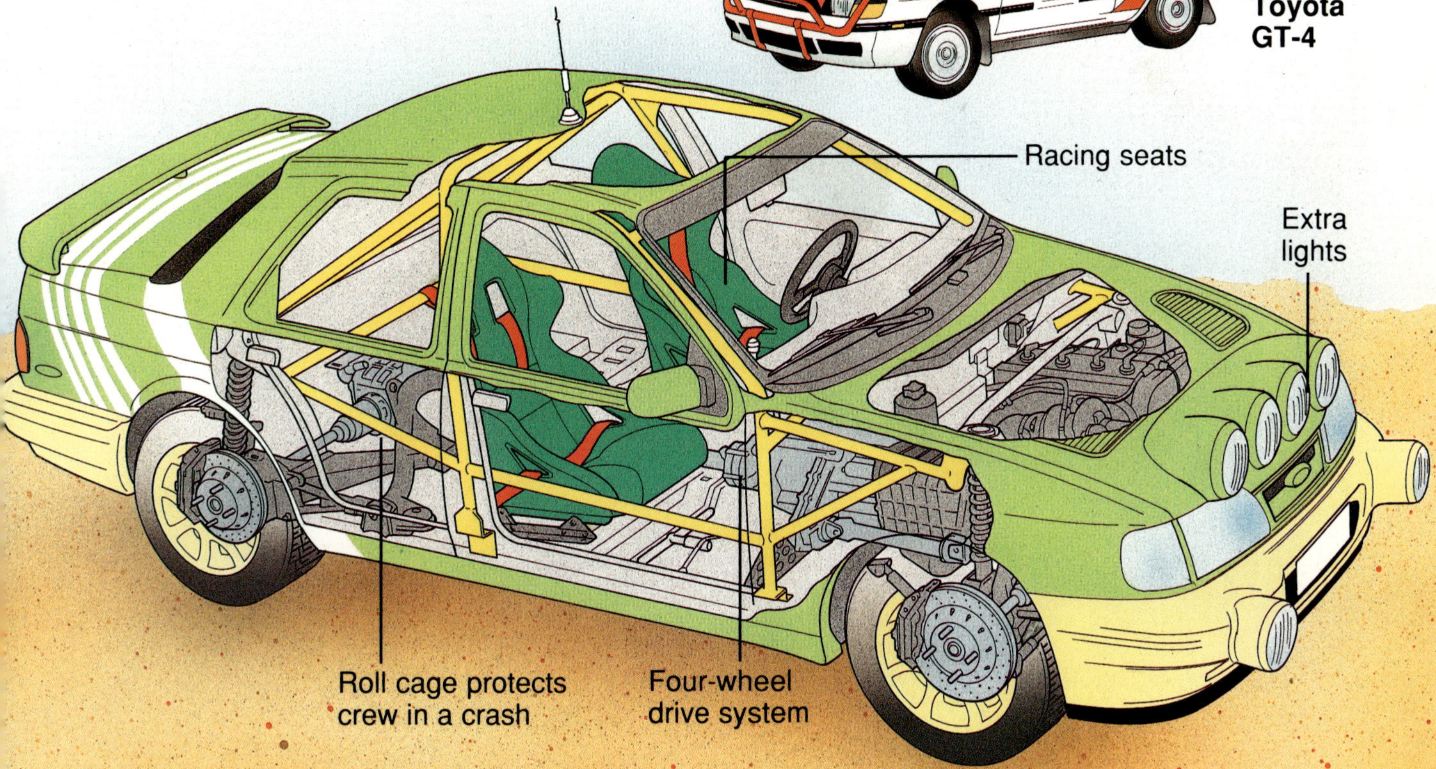

Racing seats

Extra lights

Roll cage protects crew in a crash

Four-wheel drive system

Racing to win

There is a wide variety of events in the world of motor sport, ranging from hill-climbing acceleration blasts to high-powered action on oval dirt tracks.

Whatever the type of racing though, there is one common aim for the drivers and teams who compete: they all want to take the checkered flag and win!

▽ Among the oldest events in the racing calendar is the Pike's Peak hill-climb in Colorado. The course winds its way up a mountain road, with over 150 bends to test drivers' skills. The first official race was held in 1916, when Rea Lentz drove a Romano Eight to the summit in a winning time of 20 minutes 56 seconds. Today, cars hit over 190 km/h (120 mph) as they roar up the dirt track, throwing out giant "rooster tail" dust clouds as their tires spin on the loose road surface. The present holder of the Pike's Peak record is a French-built Peugeot 405 turbocharged rally car. Equipped with giant aerofoils at the front and rear, the 405 has cut the record for the climb to less than 11 minutes.

△ Over its 20-km (12.42 mile) length, the Peak route climbs over 1,400m (4,593ft) from a start altitude of 2,851 m (9,355 ft).

◁ Rallycross is held on a mixture of tarmac and off-road surfaces, which are often rough or slippery. This makes it exciting to watch, as drivers struggle to control their cars.

△ In the United States, NASCAR (National Association for Stock Car Auto Racing) is popular. Here, hotted-up saloon cars race on banked oval tracks.

▷ Dirt-track sprint cars have huge aerofoils to keep them on the ground as they roar around loose-surfaced oval tracks. Sprint star Brad Doty drives this machine, which is based on a super-light metal tube chassis. Power comes from a high-power Chevrolet V8 engine, which is mounted in the conventional position, in front of the driver.

23

Future racers

Motor racing in the future will be just as competitive as it is today. But the emphasis for tomorrow's racers won't be just about greater speed and power.

Vehicle economy and pollution control are high on the list of world problems. So the racing cars of the year 2000 and beyond could be designed to test new sources of power in international competition. The days may be numbered for the gasoline burners, polluting the atmosphere with their poisonous exhaust fumes.

Racing cars today already use many advanced materials, including carbon fiber. Future racers could be made almost entirely of plastic. Even vital parts of engines could be made of this lightweight material.

Racing tires may start to shrink in width, heralding a return to the type of tire shapes that were common up to the late 1950s. Thin tires don't grip as well as wide ones, but their reduced "contact patch" with the road surface means they offer less resistance to movement, so a car gets slightly better fuel economy with narrower tires. A future racing formula with an eye on the environment could encourage better fuel consumption, at the cost of slower speeds on the corners.

The cars on these pages show two different design approaches for future racing machines. The three-wheel super-streamliner is powered by an engine that is fueled by liquid hydrogen. This has a pollution-free exhaust, consisting of water vapor. The more conventional grand prix racer has a tiny plastic engine behind the driver's seat. Its body weighs barely half that of a present-day racing car.

△ This sleek racing machine is based on some of the ideas of California designer Brian Baker. Its features include:
1 Single rear wheel, enclosed in the streamlined bodywork.
2 Exhaust outlet from the aircraft-style turbine engine.
3 Rear aerofoil moves with the front wings to keep the vehicle stable at high speed. An on-board computer controls the angles of these parts and can be programmed to suit any particular driver.
4 Liquid hydrogen refueling point links to tanks on either side.
5 Smooth plastic canopy. It opens to let the driver in, blows off in an emergency if the driver presses an ejection switch.
6 Driver lies in a face-first, prone position, claimed to be less tiring than the usual feet-first reclining seat.
7 Fireproof driving clothes with a built-in cooling system, to keep the driver at a comfortable temperature, even in hot sunshine.

◁ A Formula One car that looks a lot like most modern machines, but includes some unusual features. The driver's helmet fits smoothly into the roll-hoop "tower." The engine is tiny, only 71 cm (28 in) long by 25 cm (10 in) wide. It is made of a mixture of metal, ceramic and plastics. Instead of a steering wheel, the car has an aircraft-style joystick, which controls the angle of all four wheels by computer.

Racing progress

These racing cars are among the most famous in the history of the sport. Technical development has produced engines that are less than half the size of those in early racers, yet achieve speeds more than twice as great.

◁ **1912 Peugeot.** One of the best racing cars ever built. Driven to victory at the Dieppe Grand Prix by Georges Boillot at over 110 km/h (68 mph). Flat out, the car could hit 160 km/h (99 mph).

▷ **1924 Bugatti T35.** This was one of the most successful grand prix cars of the 1920s, and was winning races six years after its introduction. The wheels were made of pressed steel – most racing car wheels at the time had spokes.

◁ **1937 Mercedes-Benz W125.** Raced during the 1937 season, the W125 included design ideas that were still in use 20 years later. In its single grand prix year, the car was driven to victory seven times.

▷ **1948 Alfa Romeo 158.** Designed and raced just before World War II, the car became a race winner in 1947 and 1948. In 1950 Guiseppe Farina and Juan Fangio each won three grand prix races in 158s.

▷ **1954 Maserati 250F.** The car was driven to victory by Juan Fangio in its very first race, the 1954 Argentina Grand Prix. Three years later, Fangio became world champion, still driving the 250F.

◁ **1962 Lotus 25-Climax.** The car that changed the look of motor racing, with its monocoque body, reclining seat and mid-mounted engine. In 1962, Scottish driver Jim Clark won three grand prix races in the Lotus car. In 1963, he became world champion.

▷ **1975 Ferrari 312T.** Austrian driver Niki Lauda became the 1975 world champion in this car, beginning his winning season with a victory in the Monaco Grand Prix, a race that Ferrari hadn't won since 1955.

◁ **1988 McLaren-Honda.** Combining British chassis design with Japanese engine technology, the turbocharged McLaren proved unbeatable in 1988. The non turbo McLaren of 1989 was also a winning design.

▷ **1990 Williams-Renault FW13.** Sponsors from the worlds of beer, textiles, banking, lubricants, toiletries and cameras provided much of the $25 million needed for the Williams team's 1990 grand prix season. Renault supplied engines and technical support.

27

Facts and records

The history of motor racing is a long and exciting one. Many drivers and machines have battled on the track to cross the finish line and take the checkered flag.

The first official race was the Paris-Bordeaux-Paris event of 1895. But there were many unofficial races before this. The first known race was a 323-km (201 mile) run from Green Bay to Madison, Wisconsin. An Oshkosh steamer won this 1878 event. The first closed-circuit race was also held in the United States, in 1896. It consisted of five laps of a 1.6 km (1 mile) dirt track in a park at Cranston, Rhode Island. This time an electric car was the winning vehicle.

The oldest race still running is the Tourist Trophy on the Isle of Man. The event has been held regularly since 1905.

The quickest pit stop ever made was in 1976, when the car of ace driver Bobby Unser was refueled in an amazingly fast four seconds during the Indianapolis 500.

King of the NASCAR racers is American Richard Petty, who has won hundreds of races in his career. His best year was 1967, when he won 27 times. He was also the first racing driver to earn more than $1,000,000 a year.

Fastest-ever NASCAR qualifying speed was 342.5 km/h (212.8 mph) by Bill Elliott, driving a Ford Thunderbird in 1985. Qualifying laps are made before the race and the fastest qualifiers get the best positions at the starting line. Best of all is in front of the other cars, the "pole" position.

The Ford-Cosworth is the most successful racing engine ever made. First introduced in 1967, the engine is still used in the 1990s. The design has been continually improved, so that the latest version is still highly competitive.

▽ The Ford-Cosworth engine is a V8 design. Its cylinders are arranged in the form of a V-shape. Other engine designs have different arrangements and numbers of cylinders. The engine of the Ferrari 640, for example, has 12 cylinders arranged in two banks of six. They are both shown below.

△ A Ford-Cosworth V8 engine.

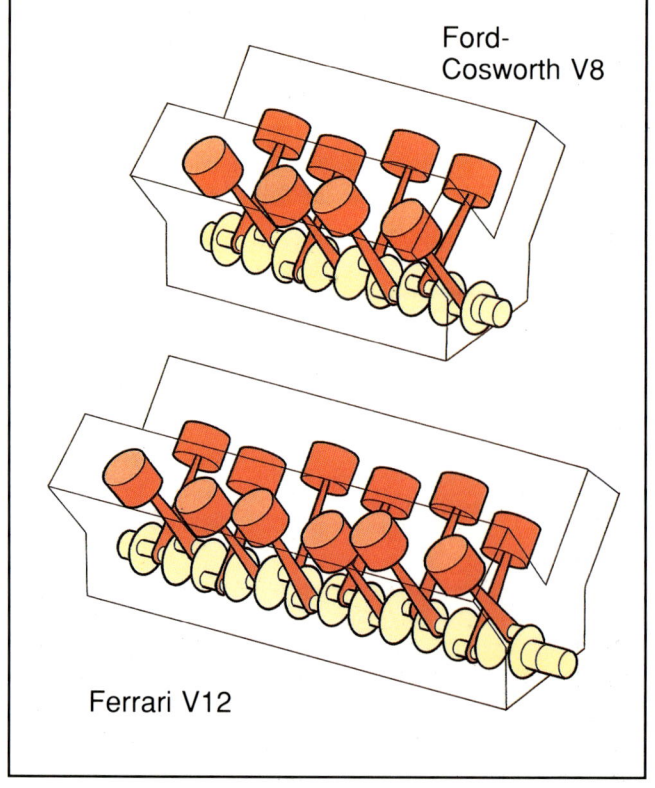

The most successful grand prix world champion was Juan Fangio from Argentina, who became world champion five times in the 1950s. Ayrton Senna holds the record for most wins in a single year, with eight victories in 1988, driving a McLaren-Honda MP4/4.

The youngest-ever grand prix winner was New Zealand driver Bruce McLaren, who won the United States Grand Prix in Florida in 1959, aged 22. The oldest winner was Italian Tazio Nuvolari, who won the 1946 Albi Grand Prix in France at the age of 53.

The most successful manufacturer is Ferrari, which has won the "constructor's prize," awarded to the season's best car, a total of eight times. In 1988 however, McLaren cars won no less than 15 of the 16 grand prix races held.

As the Le Mans drivers must race for 24 hours, the faster the cars go, the further they travel. The record for the furthest distance is held by a Jaguar XJR9, which was driven for 5,332 km (3,313 miles) during the 1988 race. This works out to an average speed of 221.6 km/h (137.7 mph) throughout the 24 hours.

The most successful make of car in the Le Mans race is Porsche, from Germany. During the 1970s and 1980s, Porsches took the checkered flag 12 times.

The longest rally ever held was from London to Sydney in 1977. The route was 31,107 km (19,286 miles) in length. The Safari Rally, held in Kenya, is the longest annual rallying event that is currently held.

△ Posters for motor sports events of the 1920s and 1930s.

▽ Drivers' helmets are as colorful and individual as their cars. Here are the helmets of five top Formula One drivers.

Gerhard Berger Austria

Thierry Boutsen Belgium

Nigel Mansell Britain

Alain Prost France

Ayrton Senna Brazil

Racing technology

This glossary explains many of the technical terms used in this book.

Aerofoil
Type of upside down wing used to keep a racing car firmly on the track at high speed. Ground-effects design shapes the body to provide downforce, as well. Between the wings and body, a racing car traveling at 240 km/h (150 mph) may well have 136 kg (300 lb) of downforce.

Aerodynamics
Science of designing machines that can slip easily through the air, with minimal drag. Designers aim for smoother, more streamlined shapes in racing cars.

Armco barrier
Metal barrier at the sides of racing tracks. Designed to absorb the impact of a vehicle traveling at high speed and prevent it from crashing into spectators.

Carbon fiber
Material that has small fibers or "hairs" of carbon added for strength. The base material is typically plastic, which can be molded and shaped as required.

Chassis
Backbone on which a car is based. Older racing cars had a steel or wood chassis. Today's cars use carbon fiber.

Clutch
Foot pedal that disengages the engine from the driveshaft. Used during gear changes.

Contact patch
The area of a tire touching the ground.

Engine size
Measured in liters or cubic inches. Describes the combined volume of all the cylinders.

Formula
Name for the set of rules and regulations that applies to each form of motor racing. It covers everything, from engine size to the weight of cars. In Formula One, weight is fixed at 500 kg (1,100 lb). The aim of the formula is to ensure that all drivers use vehicles that are roughly equal in performance, so individual skill still wins races.

Fossil fuel
A fuel derived from the remains of plants and animals. Includes gasoline, used in almost all vehicles.

Turbocharger
This device boosts engine power. Exhaust gases spin a turbine wheel. This is joined to a second turbine, called the impeller. This sucks in air, which is forced into the engine intake for more power.

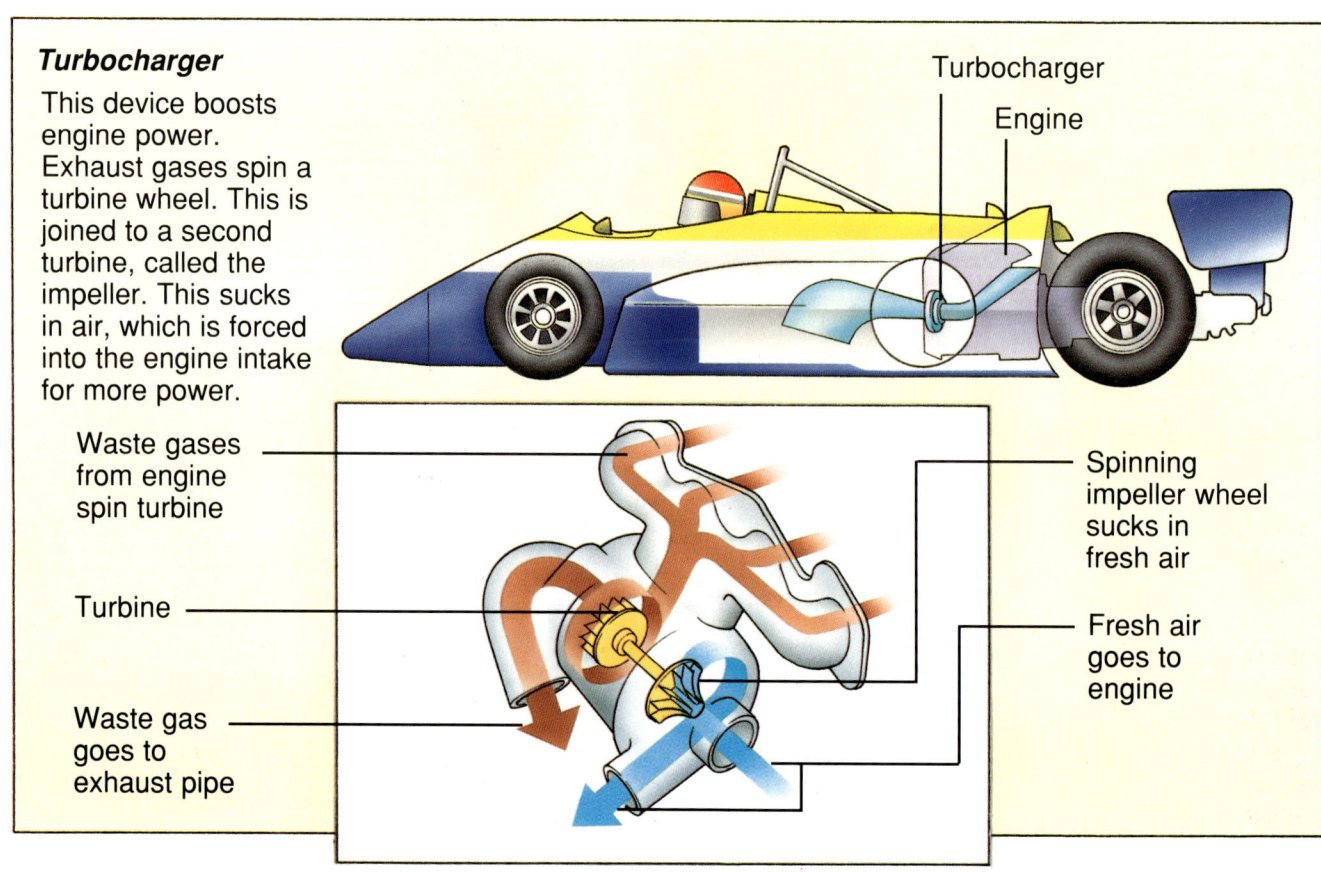

- Waste gases from engine spin turbine
- Turbine
- Waste gas goes to exhaust pipe
- Turbocharger
- Engine
- Spinning impeller wheel sucks in fresh air
- Fresh air goes to engine

30

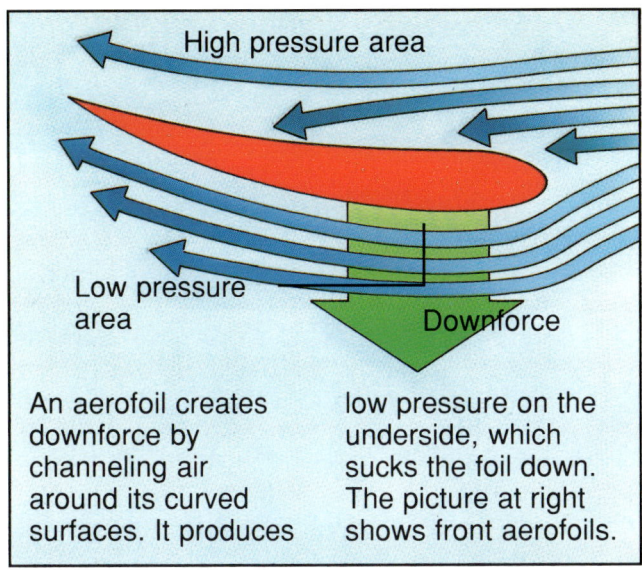

An aerofoil creates downforce by channeling air around its curved surfaces. It produces low pressure on the underside, which sucks the foil down. The picture at right shows front aerofoils.

Grand prix
The "big prize" of formula racing. In Formula One, races are presently fixed to as near 490 km (305 miles) as possible, with a two-hour time limit in the event of bad weather or other delays. The maximum number of starters in a race is 26.

Lap
One circuit around a race track. Can be of varying length, depending on the track in use.

Liquid hydrogen
Form of hydrogen made by cooling the gas far below freezing point. Liquid hydrogen used as a fuel gives no pollution. When burned, the waste product is just water in the form of a steam exhaust.

Monocoque
French word (one shell) describing the single-unit construction of a modern racing car chassis.

Pits
Areas near the starting line where mechanics service and refuel racing cars.

Roll hoop or roll cage
The roll hoop is a strong metal bar behind a racing driver's seat, designed to take the load in case of a rollover accident. Other cars, such as stock cars and sports cars, have similarly strong roll cages to protect their occupants.

Sponsorship
Form of finance. Companies supply money to racing teams in return for the right to advertise their names on the cars and use the material for publicity purposes.

Tachometer
Instrument that shows how fast the engine is running. It is not a speedometer, which shows the car's speed along the ground. The speed of the engine is controlled by pressing the accelerator pedal.

Turbine engine
Type of engine similar to the jet engines used in passenger aircraft.

△ These dry weather tires have no tread pattern, so have a big contact patch and provide maximum grip. In rain, tires with deep-cut grooves are needed to channel water away.

Index

Adelaide 9
aerofoils 16, 24, 30, 31
Albi Grand Prix 29
Alfa Romeo 158 26
  P2 15
Amon, Chris 13
Argentina 4
Argentina Grand Prix 27
armco barrier 4, 30
Austin-Healey car 12
Australia 9
Austria 29
autocross 23

banking 8, 9
Baker, Brian 24
Benetton-Ford 4
Bentley cars 13
Berger, Gerhard 29
Biasion, Massimo 20
Boillot, Georges 26
Boutson, Thierry 29
Bordeaux 6, 28
Bugatti T35 26
Brabham-Alfa Romeo BT46B 17
Brazil 4, 29
"brickyard," the 10
Brooklands 8, 9

carbon fiber 30
Chevrolet V8 23
China 20
circuits 8, 9
Clark, Jim 14, 27
clothing 18, 24
Colorado 22
Cranston 28

Darracq car 8
De Palma, Ralph 8
Dieppe Grand Prix 8, 26
Dietrich car 7
dirt-track racers 23
Doty, Brad 23
Duesenberg cars 11
du Gast, Madame 6

Elliott, Bill 28

Fangio, Juan 4, 26, 27, 29
Farina, Guiseppe 26
Ferrari 312T 27
  640 16, 28
Fiat cars 7, 14
Fisher, Carl 10
Fittipaldi, Emerson 4
Florida 29
Ford cars 13
  Cosworth 21, 28
  GT 40 13, 18
  Thunderbird 28
Formula Ford 4
Formula One 4, 5, 16, 25, 29, 30, 31
Formula Three 4
Formula 3000 4
France 4, 5, 6, 9, 12, 20, 29
French Grand Prix 7, 15
future designs 24, 25

Germany 29
Gordon Bennett Cup 8
Great Britain 8, 19
ground-effects design 16, 30
Guiness, K. Lee 9
Gurney, Dan 18

Harroun, Ray 10
Hawthorn, Mike 12

Indianapolis 10, 11
  500 race 10, 28
  Speedway 10
Isle of Man 28
Itala cars 14
Italy 29

Jaguar cars 12, 13, 19
  C-type 13
  D-type 12
  XJR9 29

Kenya 29

Lancia cars 20
  Delta 20, 21

Lauda, Niki 17, 27
Lautenschlager, Christian 8
Le Mans 5, 12, 13, 14, 18, 29
Lentz, Rea 22
Levassor, Emile 6
Levegh, Pierre 12
liquid hydrogen fuel 24, 31
London 8, 20, 29
Long Island 8
Lotus 25 14, 15, 27

Madrid 6, 7, 8
Mansell, Nigel 17, 29
Marmon 10
Maserati 250F 27
McLaren, Bruce 13, 29
McLaren-Honda cars 5, 27, 29
Mears, Rick 11
Mercedes-Benz cars 8, 12, 13
  W125 26
  W196 15
Monaco Grand Prix 27
monocoque chassis 5, 14, 31

Nannini, Allessandro 4
NASCAR 23, 28
Nazzaro, Felice 14
New York 8
New Zealand 29
Nuvolari, Tazio 29

Oshkosh steam car 28
Open-road racing 8

Panhard 6
Paris 6, 7, 8, 20, 28
Paul Ricard circuit 9
Peking 20
Petty, Richard 28
Peugeot 405 22
  1912 racing car 26

Phoenix 9
Pike's Peak 22
pollution control 24
Porsche cars 12, 13, 29
Prost, Alain 29

Renault cars 5, 6, 14
  engines 27
  Louis 6, 7
  Marcel 6
  RS 11 16
Rhode Island 28
Romano Eight car 22

Safari Rally 20, 21, 29
Sainz, Carlos 20
Senna, Ayrton 29
Silverstone 9
steam cars 7, 28
Swedish Grand Prix 17
Sydney 29
Szisz, Ferenc 14

tires 24, 31
Tourist Trophy 28
Toyota cars 20
  GT-4 20, 21
track marshals 19
turbine engines 24
turbo engine 16
turbochargers 16, 30

United States 22, 23, 28
Unser, Bobby 28
US Grand Prix 29

Vanderbilt Cup 8

Wagner, Louis 8
Waldegard, Bjorn 20
wheels, quick-change 14
White steam car 7
Williams-Renault FW13 27
World War I 10
World War II 9, 26

32